SOURDOUGH BREAD BAKING FOR BEGINNER'S

Crafting Delectable Handmade Bread
with Minimal Kneading: A Novice's
Handbook to Delicious Artisanal
Baking

Susan M Scott

Table of Contents

INTRODUCTION 5

The Joy of Handcrafted Bread 7

CHAPTER 1: GETTING STARTED WITH SOURDOUGH 9

Understanding the Basics... 9

Essential Tools and Ingredients 11

Sourdough Starter 101 14

CHAPTER 2: NURTURING YOUR SOURDOUGH STARTER
.... 19

Creating and Maintaining a Robust Starter............. 19

Troubleshooting Common Starter Issues.................. 23

Sourdough Starter Care Tips..................................... 26

CHAPTER 3: THE ART OF MINIMAL KNEADING 31

Embracing the Ease of Minimal Kneading............... 31

Techniques for Successful Dough Handling............. 34

Perfecting the Texture and Structure 37

CHAPTER 4: MASTERING THE SOURDOUGH BREAD
BASICS... 41

Classic Sourdough Loaf Recipe................................. 41

Tips for Success: 43

Shaping and Scoring Techniques... 47

Baking Tips for Beginners... 51

CHAPTER 5: BEYOND THE BASICS: EXPLORING VARIATIONS 55

Whole Grain Sourdough 55

Flavourful Additions and Mix-Ins 59

Innovative Shapes and Styles... 63

CHAPTER 6: TROUBLESHOOTING AND SOLUTIONS 67

Common Bread Baking Challenges.. 67

Tips for Perfecting Your Craft... 71

CHAPTER 7: SOURDOUGH IN YOUR EVERYDAY LIFE.... 75

Incorporating Sourdough into Meals 75

Sourdough Snacks and Treats.. 79

Using Sourdough Discard Creatively 83

CHAPTER 8: SHARING THE LOVE: GIFTING SOURDOUGH 89

Packaging and Presenting Your Loaves 89

Sourdough Gift Ideas 94

CONCLUSION.. 101

Celebrating Your Sourdough Journey 102

INTRODUCTION

Welcome to the world of making delicious sourdough bread! This guide is like a friendly companion, especially for those who are just starting. Imagine baking bread that's not like the ones you see in stores but is handmade and special. That's what sourdough is all about.

Sourdough isn't just any bread; it's like a living thing because it has natural yeast and a rich history that goes back a really long time. This guide is like a roadmap to help you become a pro at making sourdough, even if you've never done it before. Whether you love being in the kitchen or you're just curious about baking, this handbook is here to make the process easy and fun.

The best part? You don't need to spend hours kneading the dough like in traditional recipes. This guide is all about keeping it simple and stress-free. It's like a baking friend saying, "Don't worry, you've got this!" You'll enjoy the smells in your kitchen, the feel of the dough in your hands, and the excitement of watching your bread turn golden in the oven.

More than just recipes, this handbook tells stories. You'll learn about the history of sourdough, the cool science behind it, and hear from people who've already tried making their own bread.

It's like a collection of secrets and tips to make sure your baking turns out just right.

Each section of the guide helps you understand things like what a sourdough starter is, what tools you need, and how to shape and score your bread. It's like a step-by-step adventure, and you'll feel like a baking pro in no time.

This guide wants you to take your time and enjoy every step. It's not about rushing; it's about having fun and making something amazing from simple ingredients. So, if you're ready to get your hands a little floury, put on your apron, and let's start this tasty journey!

The Joy of Handcrafted Bread

In a world that's always in a rush, there's something really special about the happiness you get from making your own bread. It's not like the loaves you grab from the store – it's unique, tasty, and it comes from your own hands. This is the joy of making bread by hand, a happy nod to tradition, skill, and the pure fun of kneading dough.

The joy starts with the close connection between you and the ingredients. You begin with the basics: flour, water, yeast, and salt. Mixing these together, feeling the softness of the flour and the stickiness of the dough, brings a calm focus to the process. It's like a relaxing adventure that happens with every fold and knead.

There are all kinds of handcrafted bread, from the tangy smell of sourdough to the comforting goodness of whole-grain loaves. Each type carries your unique touch – your favorite flavours, creative additions like seeds or nuts, making it your own special creation.

The joy isn't just in the baking; it's also in watching the dough rise, seeing the golden crust form in the oven, and finally slicing into a loaf that shows off your hard work. The kitchen fills with the amazing smell of fresh bread, making everything feel cozy and happy.

Making bread by hand also brings back memories of times when families sat together to share a simple, homemade meal. Sharing a loaf you made becomes a way of showing love and care. It's a chance to connect with others by sharing something tasty and satisfying.

What's more, making bread by hand connects us to the bigger picture of where our food comes from. Choosing good, local ingredients helps support sustainable practices, making a positive impact on the environment and the communities around us.

As more people get excited about making bread by hand, there's a growing movement towards artisanal baking. People are embracing traditional methods like sourdough fermentation, understanding that good things come to those who wait.

In a world where time is often in short supply, making bread by hand encourages us to slow down, enjoy the process, and appreciate the simple joys that come from creating something special. It's a celebration of being real, going back to the basics of baking, and a reminder that happiness can be found in the relaxed joy of making something wonderful.

CHAPTER 1: GETTING STARTED WITH SOURDOUGH

Understanding the Basics

Sourdough bread is a special kind of bread loved for its unique taste and rustic feel. If you're excited about making your own bread, it's cool to understand the simple things that make sourdough special. Let's break down the key stuff that turns basic ingredients into an awesome artisanal loaf.

1. Sourdough Starter: The Magic Behind Sourdough Bread

Sourdough starts with something called a sourdough starter. It's like a mix of flour and water that grabs wild yeast and bacteria from the air. This mix makes the bread taste tangy and helps it rise without needing store-bought yeast. Making a starter takes a bit of time, but it's worth it for the fantastic flavour it brings.

2. Choosing Flour: Picking Your Flavours

The kind of flour you use is a big deal in sourdough. Most people start with all-purpose flour, but you can get fancy and use whole wheat, rye, or other special flours for different tastes and textures. It's like choosing the building blocks for your bread's flavour.

3. Water: Keeping Things Moist

Water is super important in sourdough. It affects how the bread feels and tastes. Some folks use special water to make the flavour pop, while others keep it simple with tap water. The amount of water **compared to the flour is crucial for getting the right texture.**

4. Salt: Balancing Act in Sourdough Bread

Salt does more than add flavour – it helps control how the dough rises and makes the bread structure strong. Besides its job, salt also balances out the tangy taste from the starter. Trying different kinds and amounts of salt lets you customize your loaf.

5. Fermentation: Taking Your Time

Sourdough is famous for taking its sweet time to rise. Letting the dough sit for a while is what gives sourdough its awesome taste and fluffy texture. Being patient is not just a good idea; it's a must for anyone wanting to bake artisan-style bread.

6. Shaping and Scoring: Adding Your Touch

The last step is shaping the dough and making some cuts on top before baking. Shaping gives the bread its final look, and scoring helps it expand right in the oven. This is where you can get creative, making your loaves look and taste amazing.

Getting the hang of the basics of sourdough bread is like uncovering the secrets of turning simple ingredients into a tasty work of art. It's an adventure that lets you play around, try new things, and appreciate the craft of making fantastic bread. Whether you're just starting or you've been baking for a while, sourdough opens up a world of possibilities, letting you enjoy the satisfaction of creating something truly special from the most basic ingredients.

Essential Tools and Ingredients

If you're diving into the world of baking sourdough bread, having the right tools and good-quality ingredients is like having a secret recipe for success. Let's break down the basic stuff you need to turn your kitchen into a sourdough paradise.

Essential Tools:

1. Kitchen Scale: Get Your Measures Right

Use a digital kitchen scale to measure things precisely. It helps you get the perfect balance of flour, water, and other ingredients, making sure your bread turns out great every time.

2. Mixing Bowls: Your Dough's Best Friend

You'll need sturdy mixing bowls in different sizes for mixing and letting your dough rise. Having a variety helps you handle different steps of making your sourdough easily.

3. Dough Scraper: No Mess, No Stress

A dough scraper is handy when you're dealing with sticky dough. It helps measure ingredients, shape the dough, and keeps your work area clean.

4. Banneton or Proofing Basket: Shape Up Your Bread

To get that classic bakery look, you need a banneton or proofing basket. It supports your dough during the final rise, making sure it keeps its beautiful shape and texture.

5. Dutch Oven: The Crust Game-Changer

Baking your sourdough in a hot Dutch oven gives it that perfect crispy crust. It's like bringing the bakery magic right into your kitchen.

6. Lame or Razor Blade: Fancy Bread Patterns

Before baking, you'll need to score your dough. Use a lame or a sharp razor blade to create cool patterns on the surface of your bread.

7. Oven Thermometer: Bake with Precision

Make sure your oven is at the right temperature with an oven thermometer. Having a consistent temperature is super important for getting the perfect rise and crust.

Essential Ingredients:

1. Flour: Your Bread's Foundation

The type of flour you choose makes a big difference in how your sourdough tastes and feels. You can use all-purpose, bread, whole wheat, or other special flours to give your bread its own unique twist.

2. Water: Good Water, Good Dough

Water is a big deal in sourdough. Go for filtered or mineral water to add some extra flavour. Make sure it's the right temperature to help your dough rise just right.

3. Sourdough Starter: The Heartbeat of Your Bread

Your sourdough starter is like the heart of your bread. Feed it on a regular basis to keep it healthy and active. It's got the wild yeast and bacteria that make your sourdough taste awesome.

4. Salt: The Flavour Balancer

Salt isn't just for taste; it helps your dough rise and keeps the structure strong. Use good-quality sea salt or kosher salt for that clean flavour.

5. Extra Fun Stuff: Seeds, Nuts, and More

Want to take your sourdough up a notch? Throw in some extra goodies like seeds, nuts, or dried fruits. They bring in new flavours and textures to make your bread even more delicious.

Becoming a sourdough master is a fun adventure, and having the right tools and ingredients is like having a superpower in your kitchen. As you gather everything you need, enjoy the process, try new things, and savour the joy of making your own fantastic sourdough bread.

Sourdough Starter 101

Starting your sourdough adventure begins with a special ingredient called the sourdough starter. Think of it as the "heartbeat" of sourdough bread, giving it its unique taste and fluffiness. This guide, Sourdough Starter 101, is here to help you understand, make, and take care of this crucial part in the world of fancy baking.

The Basics:

What's a Sourdough Starter?

A sourdough starter is like a living mix of flour and water that has wild yeast and good bacteria. These tiny things make your sourdough taste awesome and rise well.

Meet the Wild Yeast and Bacteria:

The cool thing about sourdough is the wild yeast and bacteria in the starter. They work together – yeast makes the bread rise, and bacteria adds that tangy flavour.

Making Your Sourdough Starter:

Ingredients:

- Flour (all-purpose or a mix with whole wheat).
- Water (without chlorine).

Step-by-Step:

- Day 1: Combine equal parts flour and water.
- Days 2-7: Throw away half and add fresh flour and water every day.
- By Day 7: Your starter should look bubbly, smell good, and be ready to use.

3. Keeping Your Starter Happy:

- Feed your starter regularly by throwing away some and adding equal parts flour and water. This keeps the yeast and bacteria happy.

Fixing Starter Problems:

1. *Liquid on Top (Hooch):*
   If your starter has a liquid on top, it means it's hungry. Feed it more often.

2. *Bad Smell:*
   If your starter smells bad, it might have bad bacteria. Start fresh with a new one.

Using Your Starter in Recipes:

3. *Check Before Using:*
   Make sure your starter looks active with bubbles and smells good before using it.

4. *Change Recipes a Bit:*
   Adjust recipes to fit your sourdough starter by changing the amounts of flour and water.

Storing Your Starter:

5. *In the Fridge:*
   If you bake every so often, keep your starter in the fridge and feed it once a week.

6. *At Room Temperature:*
   If you bake more regularly, leave your starter at room temperature and feed it every day.

Sourdough Starter 101 is like your ticket to the heart of sourdough baking. Growing and taking care of your starter is a cool journey that connects you to the ancient art of making great bread.

Remember, your starter is alive, so treat it well. With every loaf, you're not just making tasty bread; you're becoming a part of a really old cooking tradition.

CHAPTER 2: NURTURING YOUR SOURDOUGH STARTER

Creating and Maintaining a Robust Starter

Starting with sourdough is like setting out on a tasty adventure, and the key to it all is having a healthy sourdough starter. This guide will take you through the steps of making a lively starter and give you tips on how to keep it strong for making fantastic artisanal bread.

Making Your Sourdough Starter:

Ingredients:

- Use regular all-purpose flour or mix it up with some whole wheat flour.
- Get some water without chlorine.

Step-by-Step Process:

Day 1:

- Mixing the Starter
- Mix equal parts flour and water until you get a thick paste.
- Allow it to sit at room temperature, covered loosely.

Days 2-7:

- Daily Feedings
- Every day, toss out about half of your starter and add equal parts fresh flour and water.
- Look for bubbles, a rise in volume, and a slightly tangy smell.

Day 7:

- Ready to Roll

By the end of the week, your starter should be bubbling, doubling in size after feeding, and have that sour smell. Now it's ready for baking.

Keeping Your Sourdough Starter Going:

Feeding Schedule:

Feed your starter based on how often you bake. For regular bakers, daily feedings at room temperature work well. If you bake less often, keep it in the fridge and feed it once a week.

Feeding Process:

- Throw away some of your starter (about half).
- Add equal parts fresh flour and water to what's left.
- Mix it up and let it rest until the next feeding.

- Checking Starter Health:
- A healthy starter should double in size within 4-8 hours of feeding.
- It should look bubbly and have a slightly tangy smell.
- If you see a liquid layer (hooch) on top, it's hungry, so feed it more often.

Fixing Problems and Tips:

Hooch Formation:
If hooch appears, your starter needs more food. Feed it more regularly.

Bad Smell:
If it smells bad, it might have unwanted bacteria. Start fresh with a new batch.

Changing Consistency:
Adjust how much water you add to your starter based on what your recipe needs. Change the flour-to-water ratio during feedings to get the right thickness.

Using Your Starter in Recipes:

Before Baking:
Make sure your starter looks active, with bubbles and a tangy smell.

Recipe Tweaks:

Change your recipes a bit to fit your sourdough starter. Adjust how much flour and water you use.

Creating and keeping a strong sourdough starter is the starting point for awesome artisanal baking. With some attention, regular feedings, and a bit of waiting, you'll have a lively starter that makes your sourdough taste fantastic. Remember, your starter is alive, so treat it well, and it'll reward you with yummy loaves for a long time.

Troubleshooting Common Starter Issues

When you're into sourdough baking, sometimes your starter might hit a few bumps. But don't worry—this guide is here to help troubleshoot and fix those common problems.

Common Issues and How to Fix Them:

1. Liquid on Top (Hooch):

- *Issue*: There's some liquid on top of your starter.
- *Cause*: Your starter is hungry and needs to be fed more often.
- *Fix*: Feed your starter more regularly to keep it happy and healthy.

2. Bad Smell:

- *Issue:* Your starter smells bad.
- *Cause*: Unwanted bacteria might be causing the bad smell.
- *Fix:* Start fresh with a new starter, being super clean with your tools.

3. Slow Activity:

- *Issue*: Your starter isn't growing as it should after feeding.

- *Cause*: Maybe you're not feeding it regularly, the environment isn't right, or the yeast is a bit weak.
- *Fix*: Stick to a feeding routine, keep the environment warm, and consider feeding your starter more often.

4. Not Rising Well:

- *Issue*: Your starter isn't making your bread rise enough.
- *Cause*: The yeast might not be strong, or the hydration levels could be off.
- *Fix*: Adjust the feeding ratio for more water, give it more time to rise, and think about refreshing your starter more often.

5. Mold:

- *Issue*: Mold is growing on your starter.
- *Cause*: It might not be clean or have been contaminated.
- *Fix:* Toss out the moldy part, clean everything well, and consider using distilled water to be extra safe.

6. Over-fermentation:

- *Issue*: Your starter collapses or smells strong.
- *Cause*: It might be fermenting for too long or in a too warm place.

- *Fix*: Adjust the feeding schedule, keep it cooler, and maybe try a different environment.

7. Inactivity After Refrigeration:

- *Issue*: Your starter seems sleepy after being in the fridge.
- *Cause*: It might need some time to wake up.
- *Fix*: Let it warm up to room temperature and start feeding it regularly again.

How to Avoid Problems:

1. Feed Regularly: Stick to a schedule for feeding your starter.

2. Keep It Clean: Use clean tools and containers to avoid any contamination.

3. Right Environment: Make sure your starter is in a warm and stable place during fermentation.

4. Adjust Hydration: Change the water-to-flour ratio during feedings for the right consistency.

When you're dealing with sourdough, fixing little issues is part of the fun. This guide helps you understand what's going on and how to make your starter happy again. Each challenge is a chance to get better at baking your favourite artisanal bread. Enjoy your baking!

Sourdough Starter Care Tips

Keeping your sourdough starter happy is key to baking amazing bread. Here are some easy tips to make sure your starter stays lively and ready for your baking adventures.

Daily Care Routine:

1. Feed Regularly: Give your starter food every day to keep it lively and strong.

2. Discard Excess: Before feeding, throw away some of your starter to keep things balanced.

3. Enough Water: Adjust how much water you add during feedings to get the right thickness for your starter.

Feeding Your Starter:

1. Good Ingredients: Use good flour for your starter, like unbleached all-purpose or a mix of whole wheat and all-purpose.

2. Clean Water: Make sure the water you use has no chlorine, as it can affect your starter.

3. Keep It Warm: Keep your starter in a warm place, around 70-75°F (21-24°C), for consistent growth.

Observation and Adjustment:

1. Watch for Activity: Pay attention to how much your starter grows after feeding. It should double in size in 4-8 hours.

2. Adjust the Schedule: If your starter isn't rising enough or falls flat too soon, tweak your feeding schedule.

Maintaining Starter Health:

1. Use It Often: Bake with your starter regularly to keep it active and strong.

2. Store and Refresh: If you bake less often, keep your starter in the fridge and give it a couple of feedings before using it.

Troubleshooting:

1. Liquid on Top: If you see liquid on top, feed your starter more often.

2. Bad Smell: If your starter smells bad, start fresh with a new batch.

Preventive Measures:

1. Clean Tools and Containers: Use clean and sanitized tools and containers to avoid any bad stuff getting into your starter.

2. Keep It Clean: Keep your baking area clean to prevent anything unwanted from affecting your starter.

3. *Make Changes Slowly*: If you're making changes, do it gradually to give your starter time to adjust.

Taking care of your sourdough starter is a fun part of baking. Use these tips, and you'll have a strong and reliable starter ready for your delicious sourdough creations.

CHAPTER 3: THE ART OF MINIMAL KNEADING

Embracing the Ease of Minimal Kneading

Making sourdough bread is an art, and one way to make it simpler and still delicious is by using minimal kneading. Let's explore this easy method, celebrating the simplicity and great results it brings.

Traditional vs. Minimal Kneading:

Traditional bread-making usually involves a lot of kneading to get the right texture. Minimal kneading is a gentler approach, making the process easier and more accessible for everyone.

Benefits of Minimal Kneading:

This method is simple, saves time, and gives the bread a great texture and flavour. The dough gets a longer time to rest and develop its unique qualities.

Why Minimal Kneading Works:

Simple and Quick:

Minimal kneading is straightforward, making it suitable for both beginners and experienced bakers. It's a time-saver, as the dough gets more time to ferment and develop its taste and texture.

Better Bread Texture:

The longer fermentation in minimal kneading creates an open and airy texture inside the bread, giving you a chewy inside and a crispy crust.

Richer Flavour:

Sourdough is known for its complex taste, and minimal kneading lets the dough develop deeper and more nuanced flavours.

Step-by-Step Easy Guide:

7. *Mixing and Resting*: Mix the flour and water gently and let it rest. This resting time allows gluten to start forming naturally.
8. *Folding and Resting Again*: Fold the dough a few times during fermentation to strengthen it without heavy kneading.
9. *Shaping and Final Rest:* Shape the dough gently after fermentation, let it rest again before the final shaping. This helps create the right structure.

10. ***Cold Proofing:*** Let the dough proof in the fridge for a longer time. Cold fermentation adds to the flavour and texture of the sourdough.

11. ***Bake it Right***: Preheat your oven, score the dough, and bake. You'll end up with a beautiful sourdough loaf without much effort.

Tips for Success:

1. ***Be Patient***: Take it slow. Let the dough take its time to develop its special qualities.

2. ***Use Good Ingredients***: Start with quality flour and consider using a well-maintained sourdough starter.

3. ***Adjust Hydration***: Experiment with how much water you use to get the right texture for your bread.

Minimal kneading in sourdough bread-making is an easy and enjoyable way to bake. It might take a bit of patience and experimentation, but the result is a beautifully crafted loaf with fantastic flavours and textures. Enjoy the simplicity and satisfaction of making delicious artisanal bread with minimal fuss.

Techniques for Successful Dough Handling

Creating fantastic bread isn't just about having the right ingredients; it's also about knowing how to handle the dough. This guide breaks down key techniques to help you handle dough like a pro, ensuring your bread turns out delicious and beautifully crafted.

Understanding Dough Handling:

1. **Why It Matters:** Handling dough well is crucial—it affects the texture, structure, and overall quality of your bread. It's about finding the right balance between giving the dough structure and keeping it tender.

2. **Finding the Balance:** Dough handling is like a delicate dance. You want to make the dough strong through techniques like kneading but avoid overworking it.

Simple Techniques for Great Dough Handling:

Kneading:

- *Purpose*: Make the dough elastic.
- *How:* Fold, push, and turn the dough until it's smooth and elastic.
- *Tip*: Stop when the dough feels right; too much kneading makes it tough.

Folding:

- *Purpose*: Strengthen the dough without lots of kneading.
- *How*: Gently lift and fold parts of the dough during fermentation.
- *Tip*: Helps the dough rise evenly and get stronger.

Stretch and Fold:

- *Purpose*: Boost dough strength.
- *How*: Stretch a part of the dough, fold it, and repeat.
- *Tip:* Great for artisanal bread during the first stages of rising.

Shaping:

- *Purpose*: Create the final shape.
- *How*: Carefully shape the dough into a ball or loaf.
- *Tip*: A well-shaped dough looks good and rises evenly.

Pre-shaping and Final Shaping:

- *Purpose*: Make a structured loaf.
- *How*: First, make a loose shape, let it rest, and then do the final shaping.
- *Tip:* This two-step process gives the dough tension and a nice form.

Gentle Handling:

- *Purpose:* Keep air pockets and a light texture.
- *How*: Be gentle, especially with risen dough.
- *Tip:* Avoid too much handling at the end for a soft and airy bread.

Common Issues and Solutions:

Overworking the Dough:

- *Issue*: Bread is tough.
- *Solution*: Watch for dough resistance and don't over-knead.

Poor Shaping:

- *Issue*: Bread rises unevenly.
- *Solution:* Learn shaping techniques for a well-formed loaf.

Inadequate Gluten Development:

- *Issue*: Bread is flat.
- *Solution*: Make sure to knead enough or use techniques like folding.

Tips for Success:

1. **Know Your Dough:** Understand your dough—its hydration and the type of flour used.

2. **Be Patient**: Give your dough enough time to rest and rise between each step.

3. **Adjust Techniques**: Change your dough-handling based on the recipe and what you want your bread to be like.

Handling dough well is a big part of baking great bread. By practicing these techniques and getting to know your dough, you'll become a better baker, and your loaves will show off your skills.

Perfecting the Texture and Structure

Making amazing sourdough bread is more than just following a recipe; it's about understanding how to get that perfect texture and structure. This guide breaks down the key steps to help you achieve the ideal combination of a chewy inside and a crispy crust in your sourdough creation.

Understanding Texture and Structure:

Why Texture Matters:

Texture is how your sourdough feels when you bite into it—the soft inside and the crispy outside.

What's Ideal Structure:

Structure means how the air pockets are arranged inside the bread. The right structure makes the bread look good and enjoyable to eat.

Simple Techniques for Better Texture and Structure:

Choose the Right Flour:

Tip: Experiment with different flours like bread flour or whole wheat to see what you like.

Adjust Water Levels:

Tip: Change how much water you use to get the crumb texture you want. More water means a more open crumb.

Keep Your Starter Healthy:

Tip: Feed your starter regularly to make sure your dough ferments well.

Try the Autolyse Technique:

Tip: Let your flour and water sit together before adding the starter. A longer wait makes the dough better.

Bulk Fermentation:

Tip: Watch how much the dough rises and consider doing gentle folds during this time.

Stretch and Fold Technique:

Tip: Do stretch and folds during fermentation for better gluten development.

Final Proofing:

Tip: Proof the dough at the right temperature for the right time to get the structure you want.

Scoring the Dough:

Tip: Use a sharp blade to cut the dough before baking. This allows you to determine how the bread grows.

Baking Temperature and Time:

Tip: Experiment with different oven temperatures and baking times to get the crust and crumb you like.

Common Problems and Solutions:

Dense Crumb:

Solution: Adjust fermentation time, do more stretch and folds, or try changing hydration levels.

Overly Open Crumb:

Solution: Reduce hydration, proof for less time, or use fewer structure-building techniques.

Uneven Structure:

Solution: Master shaping techniques, make sure the dough is evenly distributed, and create proper tension while shaping.

Tips for Success:

- Keep Records: Write down what you do each time so you can learn and improve.
- Be Consistent: Do things the same way each time to get reliable results.
- Learn as You Go: Pay attention to each batch and adjust your techniques based on what works best for your dough.

Getting the perfect texture and structure in your sourdough bread is a journey. Use these simple tips, understand your dough, and pay attention to the details. Over time, you'll become a master at creating sourdough bread with an amazing texture and structure.

CHAPTER 4: MASTERING THE SOURDOUGH BREAD BASICS

Classic Sourdough Loaf Recipe

Sourdough bread is a classic treat with a tangy taste and chewy texture. With this simple recipe, you can make it at home in no time. Let's break it down:

Ingredients:

For the Sourdough Starter:

- 1 cup all-purpose flour
- 1/2 cup water
- 1/2 cup active sourdough starter

For the Dough:

- 3 cups bread flour
- 1 1/2 teaspoons salt
- 1 cup water (adjust as needed)
- Active sourdough starter (from the previous step)

Equipment:

- Bowls

- Scale
- Clean towel
- Dutch oven or similar baking pot
- Parchment paper
- Sharp knife for scoring

Instructions:

Sourdough Starter:

- Mix 1 cup flour, 1/2 cup water, and 1/2 cup active sourdough starter in a bowl.
- Cover and let it sit for 4-6 hours until it doubles in size.
- **Mixing Dough:**
- Combine 3 cups bread flour, 1 1/2 teaspoons salt, 1 cup water, and some sourdough starter in a large bowl.
- Mix until it forms a dough.

Kneading and Rising:

- Knead the dough for 10 minutes, or until it is smooth and elastic.
- Let it rise for 4-8 hours, doing stretches and folds every 30 minutes during the first 2 hours.

Shaping:

- Shape the dough into a loaf and place it on parchment paper.

- Cover and let aside for 1-2 hours to rise.

Preparing for Baking:

- Preheat your oven to 450°F (232°C) with a Dutch oven inside.
- Transfer the dough into the hot Dutch oven using the parchment paper.
- Score the top of the dough with a knife.

Baking:

- Bake covered for 20 minutes, then uncover and bake for 20-25 more minutes until golden.
- Cool on a rack before slicing.

Tips for Success:

Baking sourdough bread can be both fun and satisfying. Whether you're just starting or have some experience, these easy tips will help you make delicious sourdough loaves.

Choose Your Flour:

Tip: Try different flours like bread flour, all-purpose flour, or whole wheat to see what you like best.

Get the Right Moisture:

Tip: Adjust the water in your recipe for the texture you want. More water gives you a more open crumb.

Keep Your Starter Healthy:

Tip: Feed your sourdough starter regularly for better fermentation.

Be Patient:

Tip: Let your dough rise and proof for enough time. Good things take time, and your bread will taste better.

Watch the Temperature:

Tip: Your kitchen temperature affects how long things take. Plan your baking based on your kitchen's warmth.

Feed Your Starter Regularly:

Tip: Stick to a routine for feeding your sourdough starter. This keeps things stable and predictable.

Use Quality Ingredients:

Tip: Start with good flour and water. Better ingredients mean better bread.

Try Different Scoring:

Tip: Cutting your dough before baking helps control how it expands. Experiment with different patterns for a cool look.

Preheat Your Oven Right:

Tip: Make sure your oven is really hot before baking, especially if you're using a Dutch oven. A hot oven helps your bread rise well.

Learn from Each Batch:

Tip: Pay attention to what works and what doesn't. Note any changes you make and see how they affect your bread.

Quality Water Matters:

Tip: If your tap water tastes weird, use filtered or bottled water. Clean water gives your bread a better taste.

Enjoy Learning:

Tip: Sourdough baking is a learning experience. Try new things and adjust based on what you learn each time.

Use a Kitchen Scale:

Tip: Be precise with your measurements. Use a kitchen scale for both ingredients and your sourdough starter.

Adjust the Resting Time:

Tip: Experiment with how long you let your flour and water rest before adding the starter. It affects how your dough turns out.

Shape Your Dough Carefully:

Tip: Take your time when shaping your dough. A well-shaped loaf looks and tastes better.

Keep Records:

Tip: Write down what you do each time. This helps you see what works and remember successful recipes.

Share and Get Feedback:

Tip: Share your sourdough with others and ask for feedback. Different opinions can help you improve.

Have Fun:

Tip: Enjoy the process. The more you enjoy baking, the better your bread will turn out.

These tips will make your sourdough baking more enjoyable and increase your chances of baking amazing loaves. Every batch is a step forward in your baking adventure.

Shaping and Scoring Techniques

Making your sourdough bread look as good as it tastes is an art. Here's a simple guide to shaping and scoring that will make your bread both delicious and visually appealing.

Shaping:

Getting Started:

- *What*: Shape your dough into a loose round or oval.
- *Why*: It's the first step in giving your bread its structure.

Let It Rest:

- *What*: Give your dough a short rest after shaping.
- *Why:* This helps the gluten relax and makes the final shaping easier.

Final Touch:

- *What*: Shape your dough into its final form.
- *Why*: This step defines how your bread will look and ensures a nice, even surface.

Tension Matters:

- *What*: Create tension while shaping.

- *Why*: Tension helps your dough hold its shape, and using less flour prevents sticking.

Basket Time:

- *What*: Place your shaped dough in a proofing basket.
- *Why*: It keeps the dough's shape during the final rise.

Ready for Scoring:

- *What*: Turn your dough onto parchment paper.
- *Why:* It sets the stage for scoring.

Scoring:

Use a Sharp Tool:

- *What*: Use a razor or a sharp knife.
- *Why:* This allows controlled expansion during baking.

Create Patterns:

- *What*: Try different scoring patterns.
- *Why*: It adds a decorative touch and influences how your bread expands.

Get the Depth Right:

- *What*: Check that your wounds aren't too deep.
- *Why*: The depth influences how your bread rises and looks.

Single or Multiple Cuts:

- *What:* Decide whether to make one deep cut or several shallow ones.
- *Why:* It affects the shape and appearance of your bread.

Quick and Confident:

- *What*: Make swift, confident cuts.
- *Why*: This prevents dragging and tearing.

Brush or Dust:

- *What*: Optionally brush with water or dust with flour.
- *Why:* It enhances the appearance of your bread.

Tips for Success:

Practice Regularly:

Tip: Practice shaping and scoring with different doughs to improve your skills.

Adjust to Your Dough:

Tip: Change your shaping and scoring based on your specific dough's characteristics.

Embrace Flaws:

Tip: Sourdough is unique; don't worry about small imperfections.

Learn from Each Batch:

Tip: Keep notes in your baking journal. Learn from what works and what doesn't.

Enjoy the Process:

Tip: Have fun shaping and scoring. It's a creative part of making sourdough bread.

Making your sourdough bread look and taste fantastic is an ongoing adventure. With these simple techniques, you'll turn your loaves into delightful works of art.

Baking Tips for Beginners

If you're just starting your baking journey, these simple tips will help you enjoy the process and create delicious treats.

Get Your Basics:

Tip: Make sure you have essential tools like measuring cups, bowls, a whisk, spatula, and baking pan.

Know Your Oven:

Tip: Check your oven's temperature with a thermometer to be sure it's accurate.

Quality Ingredients Matter:

Tip: Use fresh and good-quality ingredients for better taste.

Measure Right:

Tip: Measure accurately using the right cups for dry and liquid ingredients.

Room Temperature is Key:

Tip: Let ingredients like butter and eggs sit out for about 30 minutes before using.

Stick to the Recipe:

Tip: Follow the recipe closely, especially as a beginner.

Preheat Your Oven:

Tip: Always preheat your oven for even baking.

Be Patient:

Tip: Don't rush the baking process. Follow recommended times and let things cool.

Learn Mixing Techniques:

Tip: Understand basic mixing methods like creaming and folding.

Play with Flavours:

Tip: Add flavour with extracts, spices, or citrus zest once you're comfortable.

Check Leavening Agents:

Tip: Make sure your baking powder and soda are fresh.

Master Butter Use:

Tip: Use unsalted butter and let it come to room temperature for better results.

Learn from Mistakes:

Tip: Don't be discouraged by mistakes. Learn and improve.

Practice Regularly:

Tip: Baking gets better with practice. Enjoy the learning process.

Try Different Baking:

Tip: Experiment with cookies, cakes, bread – explore different baking methods.

Get Dough Right:

Tip: Pay attention to dough consistency and adjust as needed.

Invest in Good Pans:

Tip: Quality bakeware makes a difference. Invest in sturdy, non-stick pans.

Decorate with Precision:

Tip: If you enjoy decorating, practice piping for a professional finish.

Connect with Other Bakers:

Tip: Join online forums or local groups to share tips and experiences.

Celebrate Success:

Tip: Take pride in your baking achievements. Enjoy the delicious results of your efforts!

Starting to bake is a fun adventure. With these simple tips, you can navigate the basics, overcome challenges, and relish the joy of baking.

CHAPTER 5: BEYOND THE BASICS: EXPLORING VARIATIONS

Whole Grain Sourdough

Discovering the world of whole grain sourdough brings a mix of hearty flavours, nutritional goodness, and the special touch of artisanal bread. This simple guide breaks down the steps to create whole grain sourdough, making it easy to understand and enjoy the process.

Understanding Whole Grain Sourdough:

1. Mixing Flours:

- **Explanation**: Whole grain sourdough uses a mix of whole wheat, rye, or spelt flours along with regular bread flour.
- **Purpose**: These whole grain flours add unique flavours, extra fiber, and good nutrition.

2. Nutrition Boost:

- **Explanation**: Whole grains keep all the good parts – bran and germ – packed with nutrients, fiber, and antioxidants.
- **Purpose**: Boosts the nutritional value and potential health benefits of the bread.

Making Whole Grain Sourdough:

1. Adapting the Starter:

- **Explanation:** Adjust your sourdough starter to work well with whole grain flour.
- **Purpose**: Whole grain flour creates a better environment for the good microorganisms.

2. Handling Water:

- **Explanation:** Whole grain flours absorb more water, affecting the dough's hydration.
- **Purpose**: Ensures the right moisture for a well-hydrated dough.

3. Take Your Time:

- **Explanation**: Whole grain sourdough benefits from longer fermentation periods.
- **Purpose**: Allows flavours to develop and makes the bread more easily digestible.

4. Soaking in Water:

- **Explanation**: Give whole grain flours time to soak up water before adding the starter.
- **Purpose**: Improves the dough's structure and texture.

5. Balancing Tastes:

- **Explanation**: Whole grain sourdough can have a stronger taste.
- **Purpose:** Experiment with balancing flavours by adjusting fermentation and salt levels.

6. Deeper Scoring:

- **Explanation**: Whole grain dough might need deeper cuts before baking.
- **Purpose**: Helps control expansion during baking.

Tips for Success:

Try Different Flours:

- **Tip**: Experiment with various mixes of whole grain and bread flours to find your favourite taste and texture.

Take It Slow:

- **Tip**: If you're new to whole grain, gradually use more in your recipes to get used to the taste.

Watch the Temperature:

- **Tip:** Whole grain dough may benefit from slightly warmer temperatures during fermentation for better results.

Add Extras:

- **Tip**: Enhance your bread with whole grains, seeds, or nuts for more texture and nutritional variety.

Be Patient:

- **Tip**: Whole grain sourdough often takes more time. Patience leads to better results.

Whole grain sourdough brings a tasty and healthy twist to artisanal baking. By grasping the steps, trying out different methods, and savouring your homemade bread, you'll enjoy the goodness of whole grains in every bite.

Flavourful Additions and Mix-Ins

Making sourdough bread is like creating a tasty canvas, and you can make it even more delicious by adding exciting flavours and textures. This easy guide explores various ways to enhance your sourdough with both savoury and sweet additions.

Tasty Savoury Twists:

1. **Herbs and Spices:**
   - **Ideas:** Add rosemary, thyme, garlic, or a bit of cayenne for a savoury kick.
   - **Result:** Your bread will have a lovely aroma and taste great with many dishes.

2. **Cheese Varieties:**
   - **Ideas**: Mix in cheddar, Parmesan, or blue cheese chunks.
   - **Result:** Enjoy a perfect blend of tangy cheese and the rich sourdough flavour.

3. **Caramelized Onions:**
   - **Ideas**: Add sautéed onions for a sweet and savoury touch.
   - **Result:** A loaf that's slightly sweet and perfect for sandwiches or snacking.

Deliciously Sweet Additions:

1. **Dried Fruits:**
- **Ideas:** Throw in raisins, cranberries, or chopped apricots for sweetness and chewiness.
- **Result:** Your sourdough gets a sweet and fruity twist.

2. **Nuts and Seeds:**
- **Ideas**: Mix in walnuts, almonds, or sunflower seeds for a delightful crunch.
- **Result**: Enjoy nutty undertones and a satisfying texture.

3. **Chocolate Indulgence:**
- **Ideas**: Add dark chocolate chunks or cocoa powder for a dessert-like treat.
- **Result:** A heavenly combo of rich chocolate and tangy sourdough.

Exotic Flavours to Explore:

1. **Citrus Zest:**
- **Ideas**: Include lemon, orange, or grapefruit zest for a burst of freshness.
- **Result**: Your loaves become bright and refreshing with a hint of citrus.

2. **Mediterranean Vibes:**

- **Ideas**: Add olives and sundried tomatoes for a taste of the Mediterranean.

- **Result:** A savoury and complex profile inspired by Mediterranean cuisine.

3. **Spicy Surprises:**

- **Ideas**: Mix in jalapeños or red pepper flakes for a spicy kick.

- **Result:** Fiery loaves that add warmth to your taste buds.

Tips for Adding Flavour:

1. **Balance the Flavours:**

- **Tip:** Make sure the added ingredients complement the sourdough without overpowering it.

2. **Gentle Mixing:**

- **Tip:** Mix in ingredients gently during shaping to distribute them evenly.

3. **Start Small:**

- **Tip**: Try new additions in smaller batches to see how they interact with the dough.

4. **Watch Moisture Levels:**

- **Tip:** Adjust moisture levels to accommodate ingredients like fruits or veggies.

5. Timing Matters:

- **Tip**: Add delicate items like herbs towards the end of mixing to keep them fresh.

Adding exciting flavours to your sourdough is like creating a tasty adventure. Whether you prefer savoury or sweet, playing with these additions will take your sourdough baking to a whole new level. Let your taste buds guide you on this yummy journey!

Innovative Shapes and Styles

Sourdough bread is not only tasty but also a canvas for fun shapes and styles. This easy guide explores different ways to make your sourdough look as good as it tastes, turning your bread into a work of art.

Basic Shapes:

Round Loaf (Boule):

- *Description:* The simple, round shape, great for beginners.
- *Look*: Rustic appearance with a crispy outside and soft inside.

Elongated Loaf (Batard):

- *Description*: Slightly longer and oval-shaped.
- *Look*: Perfect for sandwiches, with a nice crust-to-crumb balance.

Long and Thin (Baguette):

- *Description*: The classic long and slender shape.
- *Look*: Ideal for French-style bread, with a crispy outside and airy inside.

Creative Styles:

Twisted Sourdough:

- *Description*: Roll your dough into a twist for a cool look.
- *Look*: Adds a unique texture and eye-catching appearance.

Braided Sourdough:

- *Description*: Braid your dough for a fancy loaf.
- *Look*: Visually stunning with a tender, pull-apart texture.

Artisan Scrolls:

- *Description*: Roll your dough with tasty fillings and shape it into scrolls.
- *Look:* Creates swirls of flavour and a pretty cross-section.

Decorative Techniques:

Scoring Patterns:

- *Description:* Draw artistic patterns on the surface with a razor.
- *Look*: Makes your bread look even better and controls how it rises.

Flower Design:

- *Description*: Shape your dough like a blooming flower.

- *Look*: Delightful and decorative, making your bread a centrepiece.

Hollow Centre:

- *Description*: Make a ring-shaped loaf with a hollow centre.
- *Look*: Perfect for serving with dips or spreads in the middle.

Tips for Fun Shaping:

1. Add Scents:

Tip: Mix in herbs or spices for yummy smells and flavours.

2. Use Natural Colours:

Tip: Try spinach or beetroot for pretty and natural colours.

3. Personalize with Fillings:

Tip: Get creative with sweet or savoury fillings like nuts, fruits, or cheeses.

4. Practice Makes Perfect:

Tip: Keep trying and experimenting to get better at shaping.

5. Take Pictures:

Tip: Snap photos of your favourite shapes and styles for inspiration next time.

Making your sourdough look special is a fun way to be creative in the kitchen. Whether you like classic shapes or want to try something new, let this guide inspire you to make your sourdough not just delicious but also a feast for the eyes.

CHAPTER 6: TROUBLESHOOTING AND SOLUTIONS

Common Bread Baking Challenges

Bread baking can sometimes feel like a puzzle, but don't worry – even expert bakers face challenges. This easy guide breaks down common issues and gives you simple solutions to make sure your bread turns out just right.

Dough Doesn't Rise:

- *Problem:* Your dough stays flat and doesn't get fluffy.
- *Fix*: Check your yeast, make sure it's fresh, keep the dough warm, and give it enough time to rise.

Over-proofing:

- *Problem:* The dough rises too much, making a collapsed or airy loaf.
- *Fix:* Watch the proofing time, adjust according to the recipe, and shape the dough well.

Sticky Dough:

- *Problem:* The dough is too sticky to handle.

- **Fix**: Gradually add more flour while kneading, and use wet hands or oil to handle sticky dough.

Crust Issues:

- **Problem**: The crust is too thick or thin.
- **Fix**: Keep an eye on the oven temperature, preheat properly, and try using steam during baking.

Bread Collapses:

- **Problem:** Your risen dough collapses during or after baking.
- **Fix**: Don't over-proof, shape the dough well, and be gentle during shaping.

Uneven Baking:

- **Problem**: Some parts are too dark, others undercooked.
- **Fix**: Rotate the bread while baking, check your oven temperature, and cover darker parts with foil.

Tough Bread:

- **Problem**: The inside is too dense and tough.
- **Fix**: Adjust hydration, knead properly, and try the autolyse technique.

Sourdough Starter Trouble:

- **Problem**: Keeping a healthy sourdough starter is tricky.

- **Fix**: Feed it regularly, stick to a consistent schedule, and adjust hydration.

Too Yeasty:

- **Problem**: The bread tastes too much like yeast.
- **Fix**: Use the right amount of yeast, watch fermentation times, and experiment with slower fermentation.

Dry Bread:

- **Problem**: The bread turns out dry.
- **Fix**: Adjust hydration, don't over-bake, and consider adding fats like oil or butter.

Tips for Success:

Take Notes:

- **Tip**: Write down details for each bake – room temperature, proofing times, and any changes you make.

Experiment Slowly:

- **Tip**: Change one thing at a time to figure out what's causing the problem.

Know Your Ingredients:

- *Tip:* Learn about your flour, yeast, and other ingredients to make smart adjustments.

Get Good Tools:

- *Tip:* Reliable tools like an oven thermometer and kitchen scale make a big difference.

Ask for Help:

- *Tip:* Join online baking communities for advice and tips from experienced bakers.

Bread baking can be a bit tricky, but with these solutions, you can tackle common problems and bake the perfect loaf. Enjoy the journey of learning and happy baking!

Tips for Perfecting Your Craft

Making sourdough bread is like an adventure in your kitchen. Whether you're just starting or have some experience, these simple tips will help you make amazing sourdough loaves that taste like they're straight from an artisan bakery.

Use the Best Ingredients:

- ***Tip***: Choose top-notch flours and fresh water. Try different grains for more flavour.

Know Your Flour:

- ***Tip***: Flours vary, and that affects your bread. Experiment with different kinds to find what you like.

Keep a Happy Starter:

- **Tip:** Your starter is key. Feed it regularly, keep it moist, and make sure it smells good for a tasty loaf.

Watch the Temperature:

- ***Tip***: The temperature matters during fermentation. Cooler temps mean more flavour, while warmer ones speed things up. Find what works for you.

Play with Hydration:

- *Tip*: Adjust how much water is in your dough. It changes the texture. Experiment until it feels just right.

Try Autolyse:

- *Tip:* Let your flour and water sit before adding the starter and salt. It helps the dough become strong and gives great structure.

Master Folding:

- *Tip*: Forget kneading; try folding during fermentation. It makes the dough strong without being rough.

Time Your Proofing:

- *Tip:* Let your dough rise when it suits you. Longer proofing times give a stronger sourdough taste.

Get Good Tools:

- *Tip*: Invest in quality tools like a kitchen scale, Dutch oven, and a razor for scoring. They make a big difference.

Learn Scoring:

- *Tip*: Score your dough before baking to control how it expands. Try different patterns for a cool look.

Be Patient:

- *Tip*: Sourdough is slow, but that's a good thing. Let your dough rise and ferment slowly for the best flavours.

Keep a Baking Journal:

- *Tip*: Write down what you do each time. Include temperatures, how much water you use, and any changes. It helps you get better each time.

Connect with Other Bakers:

- *Tip*: Join baking communities online or locally. Share your knowledge and benefit from the experiences of others.

Love the Imperfections:

- *Tip*: Each loaf is different, and that's part of the fun. Enjoy the unique look and taste of your creations.

Becoming a sourdough pro is all about learning and having fun. Use great ingredients, understand fermentation, and don't be afraid to try new things. With a bit of commitment, you'll make sourdough that reflects your style and love for baking.

CHAPTER 7: SOURDOUGH IN YOUR EVERYDAY LIFE

Incorporating Sourdough into Meals

Sourdough bread is more than just a tasty treat – it's a versatile companion for various meals. Let's explore some easy and fun ideas to make the most of your sourdough in everyday dining.

Classic Toast and Spreads:

- *Idea:* Begin your day with toasted sourdough and your favourite spreads like butter, jams, or creamy avocado.

Gourmet Sandwiches:

- *Idea:* Upgrade your sandwich game by using sourdough. Add premium meats, cheeses, and veggies for a fancy sandwich.

Sourdough Croutons:

- *Idea:* Don't toss stale sourdough; turn it into croutons. Sprinkle them on salads or soups for extra crunch.

Sourdough French Toast:

- *Idea:* Give your breakfast a twist with sourdough French toast. Dip slices in a tasty mix and pan-fry for a tangy treat.

Artisanal Bruschetta:

- *Idea:* Make a fancy appetizer with sourdough topped with tomatoes, basil, and balsamic glaze.

Sourdough Pizza Crust:

- *Idea:* Create your pizza with a chewy sourdough crust. To make your own pizza, add your favourite toppings.

Sourdough Panzanella Salad:

- *Idea:* Mix torn sourdough with tomatoes and cucumbers for a refreshing Panzanella salad.

Sourdough Crostini with Dips:

- *Idea:* Toast thin sourdough slices and serve with dips like hummus or olive tapenade for a tasty snack.

Sourdough Bread Pudding:

- *Idea:* Turn leftover sourdough into a yummy dessert. Make bread pudding with cinnamon, raisins, and custard.

Sourdough Grilled Cheese:

- ***Idea***: Upgrade your grilled cheese with sourdough for a crisp and tangy sandwich.

Sourdough Crust Quiche:

- ***Idea***: Use sourdough as the crust for a savoury quiche filled with eggs, cheese, and veggies.

Sourdough Bread Bowl:

- ***Idea***: Create a bread bowl with a hollowed-out sourdough boule. Fill it with soup, chili, or dip for a tasty and edible bowl.

Sourdough Brunch Board:

- ***Idea***: Arrange a brunch board with various sourdough-based dishes, such as avocado toast, smoked salmon sandwiches, and fruit-topped French toast.

Sourdough Dessert Crisps:

- ***Idea***: Make dessert crisps by baking sugar-coated sourdough pieces. Serve with ice cream or fruit compote.

Tips for Success:

Play with Flavours:

- *Tip:* Try different types of sourdough, like whole grain or seeded, to add unique flavours.

Match Intensity:

- *Tip:* Think about how strong your sourdough is when pairing it with ingredients. Use milder sourdough for delicate flavours and robust sourdough for bolder tastes.

Keep it Fresh:

- *Tip:* Sourdough tastes best when it's fresh. Reheat or toast it to bring back its crispy outside and chewy inside.

Get Creative with Presentation:

- *Tip:* Pay attention to how you present your sourdough dishes. A little artistry makes the meal more enjoyable.

Adjust to Your Liking:

- *Tip:* Change the tanginess of your sourdough to suit your taste. Experiment with fermentation times until it's just right.

Sourdough bread adds a special touch to your meals, making them more exciting. From breakfast to dessert, let your imagination run wild and enjoy the unique tangy goodness in every bite.

Sourdough Snacks and Treats

Sourdough isn't just for sandwiches; it can jazz up your snacks and satisfy your sweet cravings too. Let's explore some easy and fun ideas for delicious sourdough treats that will add a tangy twist to your snack time.

Crunchy Sourdough Crackers:

- *Idea*: Turn extra sourdough starter into crispy crackers with your favourite seasonings.

Soft Sourdough Pretzels:

- *Idea:* Make soft pretzels with sourdough dough, perfect for dipping in mustard or cheese.

Toasty Sourdough Bagel Chips:

- *Idea:* Slice day-old sourdough bagels thin, toast them, and enjoy as crunchy chips with your favourite dip.

Cheesy Sourdough Straws:

- *Idea:* Roll out sourdough into strips, add cheese, and bake for savoury, cheesy straws.

Airy Sourdough Popovers:

- *Idea*: Bake light and airy popovers using a simple sourdough batter.

Crispy Sourdough Focaccia Bread-sticks:

- *Idea:* Cut sourdough focaccia into strips, brush with oil, and bake for crispy breadsticks.

Sweet Sourdough Cinnamon Rolls:

- *Idea*: Make tangy cinnamon rolls using sourdough for a delicious sweet treat.

Homemade Sourdough Doughnuts:

- *Idea*: Fry up sourdough dough for homemade doughnuts, coating them in sugar, glaze, or cinnamon.

Moist Sourdough Banana Bread:

- *Idea*: Add sourdough to your banana bread recipe for a moist and tangy twist.

Tangy Sourdough Chocolate Chip Cookies:

- *Idea:* Enhance chocolate chip cookies by adding sourdough starter for a unique tang.

Fluffy Sourdough Pancakes or Waffles:

- **_Idea_**: Mix sourdough starter into your pancake or waffle batter for a fluffy and tangy breakfast.

Nutty Sourdough Energy Bites:

- **_Idea:_** Create energy bites with sourdough discard, oats, nuts, seeds, and sweeteners for a nutritious snack.

Crunchy Sourdough Pita Chips:

- **_Idea_**: Bake sourdough pita into triangles for crispy chips, perfect for dipping.

Delicate Sourdough Scones:

- **_Idea_**: Bake tender scones using sourdough starter, adding fruits, nuts, or spices for extra flavour.

Tips for Success:

Flavourful Experimentation:

- **_Tip_**: Try different flavours like herbs, spices, or citrus zest to enhance your sourdough snacks.

Customize Sweet Treats:

- **_Tip:_** Adjust the sweetness to your liking. Some enjoy a bit of tang, while others prefer sweeter treats.

Smart Storage:

- **_Tip_**: Keep your sourdough snacks fresh by storing them in airtight containers. You can also freeze them for longer life.

Let Creativity Flow:

- **_Tip:_** Feel free to get creative. Add nuts, dried fruits, or chocolate chips to make your sourdough treats uniquely yours.

No Leftovers Wasted:

- **_Tip_**: If you have extra sourdough, turn it into delightful treats instead of letting it go to waste.

Sourdough is more than just bread; it can make snack time extra special. From crispy crackers to sweet cinnamon rolls, the versatility of sourdough adds a delicious twist to your snacking routine. Get ready to enjoy every tangy bite!

Using Sourdough Discard Creatively

When it comes to sourdough baking, one often encounters a surplus of sourdough discard—a portion of the starter removed before feeding. Rather than discarding the discard, why not channel your inner culinary artist and explore a myriad of creative ways to repurpose this tangy goodness? This comprehensive guide will unveil a host of innovative uses for sourdough discard, transforming what might be seen as waste into delightful culinary masterpieces.

Flavourful Sourdough Pancakes:

- *Concept:* Incorporate sourdough discard into your pancake batter for a tangy twist. The discard adds depth of flavour and a fluffy texture to your pancakes.

Crunchy Sourdough Crackers:

- *Concept:* Mix sourdough discard with flour, oil, and seasonings to create savoury crackers. Roll out the dough thinly, bake until crispy, and enjoy a delightful snack.

Sourdough Waffles:

- *Concept:* Elevate your breakfast by adding sourdough discard to your waffle batter. The result is a unique blend of tanginess and crispiness that will make your mornings extraordinary.

Sourdough Flatbreads:

- *Concept:* Blend sourdough discard with flour, water, and a touch of oil to create versatile flatbreads. Cook them on a griddle or in a hot oven for a quick and flavourful bread alternative.

Sourdough Muffins:

- *Concept*: Introduce sourdough discard into your muffin batter for moist and flavourful muffins. Customize with fruits, nuts, or spices for a delightful treat.

Sourdough Pretzels:

- *Concept:* Utilize sourdough discard in pretzel dough to achieve a distinctive flavour. Boil and bake for soft, chewy pretzels with a hint of tang.

Sourdough Biscuits:

- *Concept:* Add sourdough discard to biscuit dough for tender and flaky biscuits. These versatile treats complement both sweet and savoury dishes.

Sourdough Fritters:

- *Concept:* Combine sourdough discard with grated vegetables, herbs, and spices to create flavourful fritters.

Pan-fry until golden brown for a delightful snack or side dish.

Sourdough Discard Pizza Crust:

- *Concept:* Mix sourdough discard with flour, water, and olive oil to craft a unique pizza crust. The tangy undertones add depth to your homemade pizza.

Sourdough Scones:

- *Concept:* Integrate sourdough discard into scone batter for a delightful twist on this classic treat. Serve with clotted cream and jam for a delightful afternoon tea.

Sourdough Banana Bread:

- **Concept:** Combine sourdough discard with ripe bananas, creating a moist and flavourful banana bread. The tangy notes enhance the overall taste.

Sourdough Cinnamon Rolls:

- *Concept*: Elevate your cinnamon rolls by incorporating sourdough discard into the dough. The tangy kick adds complexity to this beloved sweet treat.

Sourdough Discard Crackling:

- *Concept*: Dry out sourdough discard, grind it into a powder, and mix with salt to create a unique seasoning for popcorn, roasted vegetables, or snacks.

Sourdough Discard Ice Cream:

- *Concept:* Infuse sourdough discard into homemade ice cream bases for a distinctive flavour. The tangy notes complement the sweetness of the ice cream.

Tips for Success:

Maintain Consistency:

- *Tip:* Ensure that your sourdough discard is consistently fed and healthy to maintain optimal flavour in your creative endeavours.

Experiment with Ratios:

- *Tip*: Adjust the ratio of sourdough discard to other ingredients to find the right balance for your desired taste and texture.

Flavour Pairing:

- _**Tip**_: Consider the flavour profile of your sourdough discard and pair it thoughtfully with other ingredients for harmonious results.

Storage:

- _**Tip**_: Keep your sourdough discard in a separate container in the refrigerator, feeding it regularly to keep it active and ready for use.

Record Your Creations:

- _**Tip:**_ Maintain a log of your sourdough discard experiments, noting the ratios and ingredients used. This will help you recreate successful outcomes.

Sourdough discard is not just a by-product but a canvas for culinary creativity. From breakfast delights to savoury snacks, the possibilities are endless. Embrace the art of repurposing, and let your sourdough discard breathe new life into your kitchen creations.

CHAPTER 8: SHARING THE LOVE: GIFTING SOURDOUGH

Packaging and Presenting Your Loaves

Baking the perfect sourdough loaf is an accomplishment, and presenting it thoughtfully enhances the overall experience for both the baker and the recipient. This comprehensive guide explores the art of packaging and presenting your sourdough loaves, turning your delicious creation into a visual delight and a thoughtful gift.

Choosing the Right Packaging:

- ***Consideration:*** Opt for packaging that preserves freshness while showcasing your loaf. Options include eco-friendly paper bags, bread boxes, or reusable linen bread bags.

Securing the Seal:

- ***Tip***: Ensure your packaging seals well to maintain freshness. Consider using twine, ribbon, or branded stickers for an added touch.

Personalized Labels:

- *Tip:* Craft personalized labels that include the bread's name, ingredients, and a brief note about the baking process. This offers a professional as well as a personal touch.

Bread Boxes and Wooden Crates:

- *Consideration:* For a rustic presentation, place your loaf in a wooden crate or bread box. Line with parchment paper for a charming aesthetic.

Linen Bread Bags:

- *Consideration:* Linen bread bags not only keep your sourdough fresh but also exude a classic and reusable charm. Tie with twine or ribbon for an elegant finish.

Paper Wrapping with Window Cut-outs:

- *Consideration*: Use craft paper or parchment paper with window cut-outs to showcase your loaf. This allows the recipient to see the bread's texture and crust while keeping it protected.

Gift Boxes:

- ***Consideration***: Place your sourdough in a stylish gift box with tissue paper or parchment paper. This option is perfect for gifting during special occasions.

Branded Bread Bags:

- ***Consideration***: Invest in custom-branded bread bags for a professional touch. This is an excellent option if you frequently share your sourdough creations.

Embrace Natural Elements:

- ***Tip:*** Decorate your packaging with natural elements like twigs, dried flowers, or sprigs of herbs. This enhances the presentation with a touch of nature.

Sourdough in a Basket:

- ***Consideration:*** Place your loaf in a rustic basket, either lined or directly on the base. This adds a homely and inviting touch.

Reusable Bread Wrap:

- ***Consideration:*** Use beeswax wraps or reusable cloth wraps for an eco-friendly and visually appealing packaging option.

Bread Boards:

- ***Consideration***: Present your sourdough on a wooden bread board, especially for gift-giving. It is both utilitarian and attractive.

Personalized Bread Bags:

- ***Tip:*** Consider personalized bread bags with the recipient's name or a special message. This adds a touch of uniqueness to your presentation.

Include a Recipe Card:

- ***Tip:*** Enhance the gifting experience by including a small recipe card with serving suggestions or the story behind your sourdough recipe.

Tips for Success:

Consider the Occasion:

- ***Tip:*** Tailor your packaging to the occasion. Use more festive and elaborate options for special events or holidays.

Branding Matters:

- *Tip*: If you frequently share your sourdough, consider creating a simple logo or label for a consistent and recognizable brand.

Mindful Transportation:

- *Tip:* Ensure that your packaging protects the loaf during transportation. Padding and secure seals are crucial to maintaining the bread's integrity.

Maintain Freshness:

- *Tip*: Choose packaging that allows your sourdough to breathe while protecting it from drying out. Avoid airtight containers that may compromise the crust.

Think Sustainability:

- *Tip*: Opt for eco-friendly packaging options, such as reusable bags or recyclable materials, to align with sustainable practices.

Packaging and presenting your sourdough loaves are essential elements of sharing your baking passion. Whether it's a gift or a treat for yourself, thoughtful packaging adds an extra layer of appreciation to the delicious journey of your homemade sourdough.

Let your creativity shine and turn each loaf into a work of art. Happy baking and presenting!

Sourdough Gift Ideas

The art of gifting reaches new heights when the present is not just a mere item but a labour of love and craftsmanship. Sourdough, with its rich flavours and artisanal touch, makes for a delightful and unique gift. This comprehensive guide explores a variety of sourdough gift ideas, helping you create memorable and cherished presents for your loved ones.

Customized Sourdough Starter Kits:

- *Idea:* Assemble kits with a jar of your mature sourdough starter, a personalized instruction booklet, and a selection of high-quality flour. This gift introduces others to the joy of sourdough baking.

Artisanal Sourdough Loaves:

- *Idea*: Bake a selection of your best sourdough loaves, each with a unique flavour profile. Wrap them elegantly with a personalized note detailing the flavour nuances.

Sourdough Bread Subscription:

- ***Idea***: Offer a subscription service where you provide a fresh sourdough loaf to the recipient regularly. This thoughtful gift keeps giving, delighting them with the aroma of freshly baked bread.

Sourdough Bread of the Month Club:

- ***Idea:*** Curate a monthly delivery of different sourdough bread variations. Include flavour surprises like olive and rosemary, cranberry walnut, or seeded whole grain.

Bread-Making Essentials Gift Basket:

- ***Idea***: Create a gift basket with essential tools for sourdough baking—high-quality flour, a Dutch oven, a banneton, and a dough scraper. Include a personalized recipe card for a complete package.

Sourdough Workshop Experience:

- ***Idea***: Gift a sourdough workshop or class experience. Many artisan bakeries or culinary schools offer classes where recipients can refine their sourdough skills.

Sourdough Recipe Book:

- ***Idea:*** Compile a personalized recipe book with your favourite sourdough recipes. Include tips, anecdotes, and personalized notes to make it a cherished keepsake.

Bread-Making Tools Set:

- ***Idea:*** Put together a set of high-quality bread-making tools, such as a bread lame, banneton, and a proofing basket. This gift is perfect for those who are already passionate about sourdough baking.

Sourdough Starter in Decorative Jars:

- ***Idea***: Present your sourdough starter in decorative jars adorned with ribbons or labels. This adds a touch of charm to a practical and delicious gift.

Personalized Bread Boards:

- ***Idea***: Engrave or paint personalized messages or designs on wooden bread boards. Pair them with a freshly baked sourdough loaf for a thoughtful and functional gift.

Sourdough Bread Knife:

- _**Idea:**_ Gift a high-quality bread knife specifically designed for cutting through crusty sourdough. This practical yet elegant gift is sure to be appreciated.

Sourdough Themed Apparel:

- _**Idea**_: Design or purchase clothing items like aprons, T-shirts, or tote bags with witty or artistic sourdough-related prints. A fun and stylish gift for sourdough enthusiasts.

Sourdough Bread Mix Jars:

- _**Idea**_: Layer the dry ingredients of a sourdough bread recipe in a decorative jar. Attach a recipe card with instructions for an easy and charming DIY bread-making experience.

Sourdough Picnic Basket:

- _**Idea:**_ Pack a picnic basket with a freshly baked sourdough loaf, an assortment of cheeses, spreads, and a bottle of wine. Include a blanket for a complete outdoor dining experience.

Tips for Success:

Consider Dietary Preferences:

- _**Tip:**_ Be mindful of dietary restrictions and preferences when choosing sourdough flavours or ingredients.

Personalize Packaging:

- _**Tip:**_ Add a personal touch to your gifts with custom labels, ribbons, or handwritten notes expressing your sentiment.

Include Instructions:

- _**Tip:**_ For starter kits or DIY gifts, include clear and concise instructions to ensure a successful sourdough baking experience.

Explore Unique Flavours:

- _**Tip:**_ Experiment with unique flavour combinations like chocolate cherry, garlic herb, or sun-dried tomato to surprise and delight the recipient.

Presentation Matters:

- _**Tip**_: Pay attention to how you present your gift. Thoughtful and creative presentation enhances the overall gifting experience.

Sourdough gifts are more than just bread; they represent the time, effort, and love put into creating something special. Whether you're introducing someone to the world of sourdough or delighting an experienced baker, these gift ideas are sure to make any occasion memorable. Share the joy of sourdough, one thoughtful gift at a time!

CONCLUSION

In conclusion, as we journeyed through the pages of "Sourdough Bread Baking for Beginners: Crafting Delectable Handmade Bread with Minimal Kneading," we embarked on a flavourful adventure into the heart of artisanal baking. This novice's handbook has served as a guiding light, illuminating the path to mastering the art of sourdough. From understanding the basics to embracing the ease of minimal kneading, each chapter has unfolded the secrets to creating mouth-watering loaves that carry the unmistakable stamp of handmade craftsmanship.

With a focus on simplicity and a gentle approach tailored for beginners, we demystified the sourdough process, unveiling the joy of transforming basic ingredients into delightful bread. We explored the nuances of sourdough starter creation, delved into troubleshooting common issues, and celebrated the diverse world of flavours and textures that sourdough offers.

Armed with essential tools and a robust understanding of techniques, every reader, no matter their baking background, is now equipped to embark on their own sourdough journey. Whether it's the comforting aroma wafting from the oven or the satisfaction of sharing a freshly baked loaf with loved ones, this handbook encapsulates the essence of the deeply rewarding and fulfilling experience that is sourdough baking.

As you knead, shape, and savour the fruits of your newfound skills, remember that each loaf tells a story – a story of patience, passion, and the simple joy of creating something beautiful from scratch. May the knowledge gleaned from these pages continue to inspire your culinary endeavours, encouraging you to embrace the art of artisanal baking with open arms.

So, go forth with confidence, armed with the knowledge and enthusiasm to craft delectable sourdough loaves. Let the rhythm of minimal kneading and the alchemy of fermentation guide your hands as you bake your way into the heart of this timeless tradition. May your kitchen be filled with the comforting aroma of freshly baked bread, and may each slice bring you the pure satisfaction that comes from creating, sharing, and savouring the art of sourdough.

Celebrating Your Sourdough Journey

The art of making sourdough bread is a journey that combines science, patience, and creativity. From capturing wild yeast to crafting a perfectly crusty loaf, each step is a testament to the symbiotic relationship between the baker and the dough. Celebrating your sourdough journey is not just about the final product; it's about relishing the process, the challenges overcome, and the unique flavours that emerge. Let's explore how to savour and commemorate your sourdough adventure.

Capturing the Wild: The Magic of Fermentation

The journey begins with capturing wild yeast from your environment. This step, often called creating a sourdough starter, is a celebration of nature's microbial diversity. Reflect on the initial excitement of seeing bubbles form and the transformation of simple flour and water into a living, breathing culture.

Nurturing the Starter: A Living Organism

Your sourdough starter is more than just a leavening agent; it's a living organism with its own personality. Celebrate the moments of daily feedings, witnessing its rise and fall, and understanding its unique aroma. Consider giving your starter a name, and recognize the role it plays in your sourdough success.

The Art of Dough: From Mixing to Shaping

Mixing flour, water, and salt may seem straightforward, but the subtle dance of hydration, autolysis, and fermentation is where the magic happens. Celebrate the tactile joy of kneading and shaping your dough. Each fold and turn is a small victory, bringing you closer to the perfect loaf.

Rising to the Occasion: Patience in Fermentation

Sourdough is a testament to patience. Celebrate the slow fermentation process that develops complex flavours and improves digestibility. As you watch the dough rise, savour the anticipation of the final result.

The Perfect Bake: A Culmination of Effort

When your shaped dough transforms into a beautifully baked loaf, it's time to celebrate your hard work. The golden crust, the audible crackle as it cools, and the aroma that fills your kitchen are all rewards for your dedication.

Breaking Bread: A Communal Celebration

The joy of sourdough is best experienced when shared. Invite friends and family to celebrate your sourdough journey with a communal meal. Breaking bread together symbolizes the communal spirit of baking, fostering connections and creating lasting memories.

Experimentation: Embracing Creativity

Celebrate the freedom to experiment. Try different flours, hydration levels, and flavour additions. Whether it's incorporating seeds, nuts, or herbs, each experiment adds a unique chapter to your sourdough story.

Documenting Your Progress: A Personal Chronicle

Create a sourdough journal to document your journey. Record recipes, observations, and even the occasional mishaps. Looking back at your progress can be a source of inspiration and a reminder of how far you've come.

Sharing the Love: Community and Online Platforms

Join online sourdough communities to connect with fellow bakers. Share your successes, seek advice for challenges, and celebrate the diversity of sourdough around the world. The collective passion for sourdough is a global celebration in itself.

Continuing the Journey: Never-ending Learning

The celebration of your sourdough journey is ongoing. Embrace the fact that there is always more to learn and explore. Whether it's mastering a new technique or discovering a unique flavour profile, each bake contributes to your growth as a sourdough enthusiast.

In conclusion, celebrating your sourdough journey is not just about the end result; it's about honouring the process, the learning, and the community that surrounds this ancient tradition. So, raise a slice to the microbes, the flour, the process, and most importantly, to the joy of baking and sharing your sourdough creations.

Made in United States
Troutdale, OR
11/25/2024

25259530R00060